Leather Wo
Made Easy

Step-by-step Guide to Leather Working and Leather Crafting for Beginners

Leather working made easy

Introduction

Mary Allen felt that working with leather would be her last option since her leather handbags had worn out so badly over the years. Taking the bags for repair drained her pockets because the bag repairs would give out after a while. Therefore, she decided to take matters into her hands!

She went on to do some research to find if she could do the repairs herself, but all was in vain. Reading her complaints and those of others on a Facebook group[1] inspired me to write this book.

Like Mary Allen, buying expensive leather products only to discard them can be discouraging. With this book, you will learn how to maintain your leather products and make them from the comfort of your home!

Here is a noteworthy tidbit of information:

A study[2] shows that the demand for leather products in the USA will expand to \$13.1 billion in 2022, which is huge,

---

[1] https://facebook.com/groups/847305112074956/

[2] https://www.prnewswire.com/news-releases/us-demand-for-leather-and-fur-products-to-reach-13-1-billion-in-2022--300648861.html

Leather Working Made Easy

right? That means if you are a leather craftsman with an entrepreneurial mindset, you can seize the opportunity to create more leather products to sustain yourself financially and satisfy the need for a certain product you have in mind.

As you consider getting started, you may have questions like:

Is it hard to learn leatherworking?

What do I need to start leatherworking?

How do I work with leather tools?

What can I make with leather?

How much can I make with leatherworking?

This book will address these questions and many more you may have regarding leatherworking and crafting.

This book will also give you a detailed step-by-step guide on creating leather projects for domestic and commercial purposes.

You being here means you want to learn:

How to work with leather

The tools you need for leatherworking and crafting

Leather working made easy

How to acquire skills to help you complete your projects successfully.

How to identify the best leather material for each project

And much more

Even if this is your first time working with leather, and you want to add leatherworking and crafting to your skills repertoire, this is the book for you.

Let us begin.

Leather Working Made Easy

Table of Contents

Introduction _____ **2**

Chapter 1: Understanding Leatherworking and Crafting _____ **9**

Types of Leather _____ 9

Chapter 2: Tools Used in Leatherworking and Crafting _____ **16**

Leather Stamping Tools _____ 26

Custom Leather Stamping Tools _____ 28

Markers and Pens _____ 30

Chapter 3: Stitches Used In Leatherworking _____ **32**

Chapter 4: Setting Up Your Leather Working WorkSpace _____ **39**

Chapter 5: Getting Started on Leather Working and Crafting _____ **43**

Preparing The Leather _____ 43

Leather working made easy

Cutting The Leather _____ 44

Leatherworking and Crafting Techniques _____ 44

Chapter 6: Leather Pyrography _____51

Leather Burning Tool _____ 52

Designs Transfer Materials _____ 52

Chapter 7: Leather Care And Maintenance Tips_____57

Chapter 8: Leatherworking Projects_____ 60

Project 1: Leather Tool Case _____ 60

Project 2: Leather Tote Bag _____ 64

Project 3: Carved Leather Earrings _____ 67

Project 4: Leather Bracelet_____ 70

Project 5: Stamped and Dyed Leather Belt ____ 72

Project 6: Pyrographed Leather Wallet_____ 75

Project 7: Leather Phone Case _____ 78

Project 8: Leather Sunglasses Case _____ 80

Leather Working Made Easy

Project 9: Leather Sandals_____ 83

Project 10: Simple Leather Pouch _____ 88

Project 11: Pencil Case _____91

Project 12: Leather Key Holder _____ 94

Project 13: Leather Plant Hanger _____97

Project 14: Leather Dog Collar _____100

Project 15: Leather Mouse Pad_____103

Project 16: Leather Cord Keeper_____106

Project 17: Leather Bottle Holder _____108

Project 18: Leather Valet Tray _____ 111

Project 19: Leather Double Wrap Cuff_____ 113

Project 20: Leather Clutch Bag_____ 116

Project 21: Leather Flask_____120

Project 22: Minimalist Wallet _____ 122

Project 23: Leather Pen Case _____ 124

Leather working made easy

Project 24: Leather Flip Flops _____127

Conclusion _____ 131

Leather Working Made Easy

Chapter 1: Understanding Leatherworking and Crafting

The first important question we need to answer is this, what is leatherworking and crafting?

Leatherworking is simply the practice of making things from leather.

Leather crafting involves making works of art from leather using shaping or coloring techniques.

The use of leather dates back to the stone age period in 5000 BC, whereby early men used the material for shelter, shoes, and apparel. During that period, humanity survived by hunting animals and using the animal parts such as hides and furs for clothing and shelter needs.

The practice has evolved over the years, and today, you can find leather in many forms, colors, and uses across the globe, with products such as wallets, handbags, shoes, belts, apparel, wristwatch straps, and many others flooding the markets.

Types of Leather

When purchasing leather, you need to understand the four main basic types, namely;

Full-grain leather

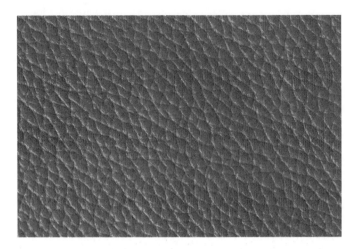

This is the most popular type of leather. Its main characteristics are smooth and luxurious with very few defects. The grain of this fine leather is intact; hence, its fibers are usually long-lasting and stable, which means the leather does not wear out easily. Also, the grain allows airflow in and out of the material, making the leather have less moisture from any prolonged contact, be it surfaces or human contact.

There are two types of full-grain leather: *Aniline* and *semi-aniline*. Aniline leather is richer in quality than semi-aniline leather and is only dyed using soluble dyes. On the other hand, Semi-aniline has a thin coat that keeps it from wearing out and staining.

Leather Working Made Easy

Full-grain leather is common in the production of high-end items such as apparel, shoes, furniture, and bags.

Pros of full-grain leather

- It does not wear out over time; instead, it becomes more beautiful as it ages.

- The leather is original and unique since it is made from the top layer of the hide, meaning that it maintains all the scars and marks the animal had.

- It is the strongest type of leather, meaning it is more durable than the rest. It also does not peel, tear, or crack, making it worth investing in.

- As the leather ages, the color also changes, which is a unique characteristic in leather.

- It is easy to maintain as you only need to wipe off the dust often and store the leather in a cool, dry place to keep it soft.

Leather working made easy

Top-grain leather

This type of leather is the second most popular. Its coat is thinner than full-grain leather as its layer is detached, making it easy to bend. The top of the top-grain leather is usually sanded to remove any defects in the finish, which is why the material is softer than full-grain leather. While sanding gives the leather a nice finish, it also takes away a lot of its strength and some of its water-repellent qualities.

However, its softness and flexibility are an added advantage as the leather is used in expensive leather goods like bags, shoes, belts, and wallets. Most people prefer buying it due to its availability.

Pros of top-grain leather

- It is easier to work with than the full-grain leather since it is flexible, which makes the leather ideal for a range of products.

- It is less expensive than full-grain leather.

Genuine leather

Genuine leather is made from any part of the hide; in other words, the left-overs of the leather after making high-end products e. Its quality is low, which is why it undergoes processes such as sanding to remove any defects, thereby altering its preferred qualities. Products made from genuine leather are not as appealing to the eyes as high-quality leather products and are not durable as they wear out easily.

However, this type of leather is affordable and easily available to most people.

Pros of genuine leather

- It is more affordable and available than full-grain and top-grain leather.

- It enhances the use of left-over hides for leather manufacture instead of wasting them.

Bonded leather

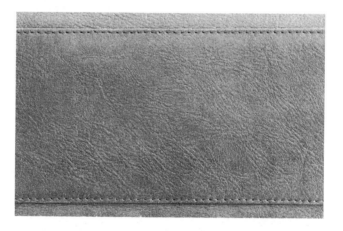

Bonded leather is also known as lesser-known grain leather. It is made up of leather scraps cut and bonded together using latex to better its functionality and aesthetic qualities. To give it color, bonded leather is painted and sometimes pressed to give it a particular leather style.

Leather Working Made Easy

Bonded leather is usually more affordable and also readily available in stores.

Pros of bonded leather

- It is readily available in leather stores and is more affordable compared to the rest.

- It has a smooth texture.

- You can get it in a variety of colors and styles.

Now that you understand leatherworking and crafting and types of leather, let us discuss the tools you need to get started in the next chapter.

Leather working made easy

Chapter 2: Tools Used in Leatherworking and Crafting

Various tools are important when working with leather. As a beginner, you may only need tools for light-weight leather tooling, but as you progress, you may need to acquire more tools that will help you develop your skills as you create more complex projects.

Here are tools commonly used in leatherwork and craft.

Awls

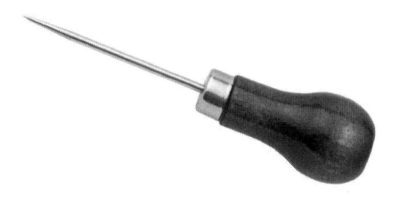

A leather awl is a handheld tool that has a sharp point either straight or slightly bent, which you can use for marking, sewing, punching holes, or piercing leather. You can especially use it to punch holes on leather before passing the stitching needle through to make sewing easier.

Craft knife

A craft knife guarantees a clean-cut and a better view of the leather parts you want to cut. The good thing is that you can also use it to cut thick leather, unlike scissors which you can only use for thin leather.

Leather working made easy

Leather stitching needles

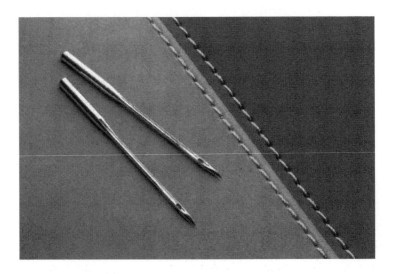

Leather stitching needles help guide thread through pre-made holes on the leather when stitching. Since you mostly pass the needle through already-punched holes, your stitching needle do not need to be overly sharp.

Leather hole punch

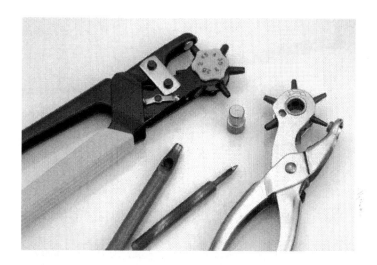

Leather hole punches come in different sizes, shapes, and widths, but each has a specific role. For example, small punches are best for making holes for stitching through, while bigger punches are ideal for creating holes big enough for things like belts or watch bands.

Synthetic thread

Leather thread helps join leather pieces through stitching. Having the right leather thread is extremely important since it makes leather stitching work easy. The best synthetic thread to use is bonded nylon available in many colors and is usable for both hand and machine sewing.

Overstitch wheel

Also called a tracing wheel, an overstitch wheel is a tool with multiple teeth on its wheel. You just roll the wheel along your leather to create neat and uniform stitches in a straight line.

Cutting mat

You also need cutting marks all over your working table, which is why you must have a cutting mat that plays the role of protecting your table as you cut your leather pieces.

Some cutting mats have griddled lines on them; these lines come in handy when measuring and laying out the leather; hence, they double as a measuring tool and a straight edge.

Edge burnisher

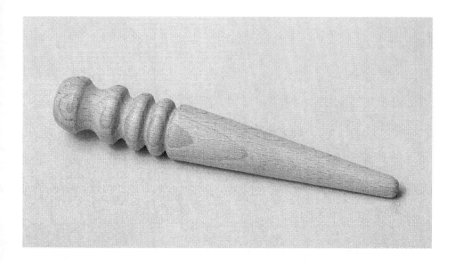

Leather burnishing involves smoothening the rough edges of leather to give it a finished look. To do this, you use an edge burnisher. When you rub the burnisher on the rough edges, friction occurs, melting the fibers of the edges to give them a smooth, fray-resistant finish.

Leather working made easy

Mallet

A mallet looks like a hammer, but unlike a hammer, its head is commonly wooden and occasionally plastic or made of rawhide. Its most common use is punching holes on belts, bags, saddles, and other leather goods. For starters, purchase these two types of mallets.

- A rawhide mallet for general use on leatherwork.
- A wooden or rubber mallet for heavy tasks like punching holes through stacks of leather with a chisel.

Groover

A groover will help create a straight groove in your leather to guide you when stitching. The groover has a cutting head and a cutting arm that will help you make a straight groove. You simply place the cutting arm next to the edge of your leather, then drop the cutting head and drag the groover to create the stitching line.

Swivel knife

A swivel knife has a chisel-edged blade used for leather carving and cutting leather.

Leather Stamping Tools

Leather stamping tools are tools used to add patterns into the leather by applying force to one end of the tool. They are usually made from metal and are about 6 inches long, with shapes carved into their base. These shapes are the ones transferred into the leather. When purchasing or using leather stamping tools, consider the following factors:

Leather Working Made Easy

- Stainless steel stamps are more durable and easiest to maintain.

- Keep your stamps clean and the base free of rust and damage. Also, ensure that no design elements are missing.

- Go for high-quality stamps as they produce quality work overtime.

- Stamps produced in masses and sold in bulk at retail premises are the most cost-friendly ranging between $5 and $15.

There are two main categories of stamping tools;

Shape stamps

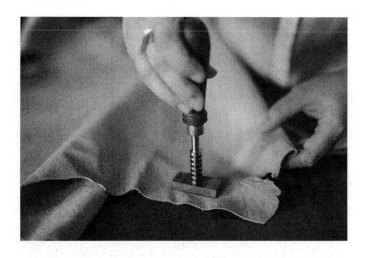

If you want to make shapes, patterns, or geometric designs, shape stamps come in handy as they have unique designs such as flowers, leaves, hearts, and many other designs you can use. You can also use shape stamps with other stamps to have create more unique designs.

Carving stamps

Unlike shape stamps, carving stamps work tandemly with a swivel knife to create more detailed and noticeable designs on leather.

Custom Leather Stamping Tools

Custom leather stamping tools are created using 3D printers and made out of steel, brass, or resins. The good thing is that these stamps allow for individuality, thanks to their customization to your needs. Instead of using the common shapes readily available, you can also have a custom-made mark or logo on the stamping tools.

Leather glue

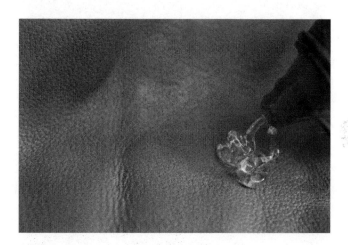

Leather glue helps bond leather pieces together either temporarily or permanently.

You can still make your stitches without tacking with glue first, but the process is struggle-full, so consider having one. A temporary bond holds pieces together before sewing, while a permanent bond holds leather pieces together for later integration into a finished piece.

Markers and Pens

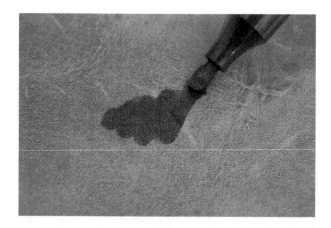

You can also use leather markers or pens to make cut marks and write on your leather. Here are examples of markers and pens;

Touch up pen

A touch-up pen can help you cover or fix any wear marks on leather so that they are less visible. They come in various colors to help you match the color of the leather products you want to fix.

Leather marker

Leather markers have applicators that help them add visual design on leather products such as shoes; they also come in various colors.

Leather Working Made Easy

Silver marking pen

This kind of pen leaves visible, silver cut marks on leather; these marks are wipeable to ensure it does not leave a permanent mark on your leather.

Leather dye pens

Leather dye pens help cover areas of dyed leather that may be scratched or have minor repairs. They also come in many different colors so that you do not have trouble selecting a color that matches the area you want to fix.

Now let's focus on the common stitches used in leatherworking:

Leather working made easy

Chapter 3: Stitches Used In Leatherworking

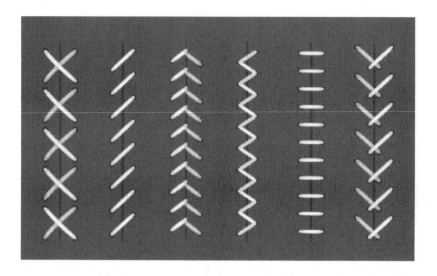

When stitching leather, you need to have at least two stitching methods you can choose from to create a unique finish. Here are different ways you can stitch leather.

Single stitch

A single stitch looks similar to a saddle stitch, only that you only require to use one needle. There are two ways you can make a single stitch;

- First, place one end of the thread through the needle eye.

Leather Working Made Easy

- Take the other end of the thread and wrap it around at least three times.

- Next, pull up the wrapped thread past the eye of the needle and the other end of the needle. The result is a knot at one end of the thread.

- Finally, lock the thread through the needle eye, and with that, you can make your single stitches onto the leather. The knot allows you to pull the thread without pulling it through the leather.

The other way you can do it is by placing the thread through the needle eye and leaving about two inches hanging on one end, so it does not go all the way through the eye. Hold the excess thread piece while stitching to keep it from passing through the leather.

Stitching using this method asks that you start sewing from the second hole, run the thread through, go back to the first hole, then skip to the third hole. Keep doing this until you complete your stitching.

Cross stitch

A cross stitch looks like an x across the leather. Here is how to do it.

Leather working made easy

- First, use your leather punch to make holes parallel to where you will do the stitching. Make sure you have an equal amount of thread on both sides.

- Make a line parallel to the top through the first two holes for more secure stitching.

- Next, pass the needle across the other side and diagonal to the third hole and pull your thread through. Keep doing the same with the other holes.

- From the backside of your leather, cross the threads through the parallel holes making sure that each cross starts on the same side for a uniform appearance.

Saddle stitch

A saddle stitch is the strongest for leather goods and the most beautiful. Here is the method for making a perfect saddle stitch.

- First, punch some stitching holes using your leather punches or stitching chisels. Next, measure your thread depending on the thickness of the leather you are using and pull it through both needles as you do with the single stitch.

Leather Working Made Easy

- Pull your needle on your right hand through the first hole so that you have an equal amount of thread on both sides of the leather.

- Next, pull the needle on your left hand through the second hole, ensuring both needles form a cross shape. Let the right needle be at the front, with the left behind the right.

- Pull the thread a bit tightly until the tail pulls through the hole. Keep repeating the same until you complete the stitching.

Box stitch

In this case, the leather is in a box-like shape throughout the stitching. A box stitch is simple as you only begin by pulling the needle through the front and bottom holes of the two leather pieces, then go down a hole back and forth until you are through.

Butt stitch

This stitching type is popular with steering wheels and objects that need wrapping with leather. Just like a saddle stitch, a butt stitch also requires two needles.

Leather working made easy

- First, punch holes through the leather pieces, making sure the holes align on both pieces, then thread both needles.

- Next, push one of the needles through the top of the right leather piece, then through the underside of the left leather piece.

- After that, pull the right needle through to the left side.

- Pull the left needle from the first hole through the second hole and the right piece side hole.

- When you get to the end, attach both threads through the bottom.

French seam stitch

A French seam stitch is common in car seats. If you are using thick leather for your project, this stitch may be difficult to work with as you have to start stitching from the inside, then flip the material back over; preserve this stitch for thick leather materials.

- Start by punching holes through the two pieces with the smooth sides facing each other. Since you cannot

Leather Working Made Easy

glue the smooth sides together, use binder clips instead to hold the pieces together when punching.

- Next, do a single stitch from top to bottom.

- After that, spread the stitched leather apart with the smooth side facing down, then use glue to attach a piece of leather into the middle of the layers.

- Once done, use a groover to mark lines at the sides of the middle layers, then punch holes on each side, making sure the holes pass through the leather and the layers.

- Single stitch the two lines, and you will have made your French stitch seam.

Baseball stitch

It is known as a baseball stitch because its first use was baseballs.

- Place two pieces of leather next to each other with the smooth sides facing up and make two parallel lines running down each piece near the middle of the two pieces. You can then punch-stitch the holes using an awl or punch.

Leather working made easy

- Pull both needles through the holes from the back, then let the right needle go under and through the second hole of the left side. This creates a diagonal line that ends at the center of both pieces.

- Do the same with the left needle to form a diagonal line similar to the right one.

- Now the diagonal lines form a v shape, and you can repeat the process until you reach the end. Cut and burn the excess thread.

With that knowledge on the common types of stitches you can use for hand stitching leather, let us learn some important tips for setting up your workspace.

Leather Working Made Easy

Chapter 4: Setting Up Your Leather Working WorkSpace

As a beginner, it is important to understand the following leatherworking and crafting tips before you can even fill up your working space with tools and materials.

Lighting and Ventilation

The first thing to do is make sure your workspace has enough light to help you make fine cuts on the leather. To reduce the shadows, use fluorescent lights or LED shop light panels. You can also paint your workspace with reflective paint so that the light will bounce off the wall and floor, contributing to uniform lighting.

Also, let fresh air flow in your workspace because some leather projects will need chemicals such as dyes to achieve some styles, and inhaling these chemicals in an enclosed room may not be good for your health. In general, leatherworking does not have many occupational hazards, but it is good to err on the side of caution and care.

Buy The Best Tools You Can

Quality tools are certainly expensive and produce quality work, but you do not have to purchase the costliest ones right

Leather working made easy

away. It all depends on how much you are ready to spend and the tools you need to purchase for the project you have in mind.

For example, you do not need to buy an expensive mallet because both cheap and expensive ones serve the purpose well. However, you need high-quality cutting and sewing tools, which is why you should buy the best you can afford.

Organize Your Working Space

Having tools and materials all over the place will lead to messy work. You may end up damaging items with misplaced needles or cutting tools or even end up cutting yourself. To keep this from happening, buy yourself a simple toolbox and arrange each tool according to its type for easy access. For example, you can have a tray for cutting tools, one for stitching tools, and another for marking tools. Also, clear up after each stage of your project.

This is a very useful tip to consider as a beginner. It helps you identify which stage feels like a struggle. For example, you have preparation, marking and measuring, cutting, stitching, and finishing. Do each of these different stages independently, one at a time, then clean up afterward. That way, you maintain tidiness as well as become more efficient.

Leather Working Made Easy

Have a working surface that fits

Ensure your working surface does not damage your tools when cutting through the leather to size. You can lay a self-healing mat on top of your working table to protect the blades of your knives when cutting your leather.

Also, when using tools such as a mallet, consider setting a granite slab on top of your working surface to provide a hard surface for pounding. Another trick you can use is setting a plastic board under the leather when punching holes to protect your punching tools from damage.

Careful when cutting

The cutting tools must always be sharp for fine cutting, especially when handling thick leather. That means it is easy to injure your skin while cutting. To avoid injuring yourself, always cut away from your body and avoid using bent or broken sewing tools when stitching leather. Also, be careful when grasping any sharp objects.

Clean up after

Finally, once done with your leathercrafting for the day, remember to clear up your workspace and put all the tools away into the toolbox or any space you have preserved for your tools.

Leather working made easy

Cleaning up keeps the tools from causing damages, such as injuring your feet, hands, or any other part of your body. Also, if you have children around, cleaning and tidying your workspace helps you avoid the risk of your kids finding these tools and injuring themselves.

Learn hand stitching

Hand stitching is not as difficult as it seems. It does not matter if your project is large or small; hand-stitching can be simple. The good thing with making your stitches by hand is that the stitches last longer and make for a beautiful project.

However, not all hand stitches are durable. Some stitching methods, like lock stitching, are not ideal for leatherworking as they are not durable. When it comes to hand-stitching, saddle stitching is the strongest way to stitch leather goods as it produces a more durable stitch than machine stitching. The main reason is that if a thread rips on the saddle stitch, the only area affected is the rip area. That means the remaining stitches are still intact, which is advantageous because you only have to repair the affected area rather than replace the entire stitching line.

Now that you know what to keep in mind as you set up your workspace, let us learn the techniques used in leatherworking and crafting.

Leather Working Made Easy

Chapter 5: Getting Started on Leather Working and Crafting

This chapter will focus on the techniques used in leatherworking so you can understand what working with leather entails.

Before we even get to the techniques and skills, we need to prepare and cut the leather. Let us see how.

Preparing The Leather

First, purchase your leather from a leather house, not a fabric store. In a leather house, you will find experts in leather types and different types of leather.

After purchasing your leather, the next step is to have the designs or images you want to transfer to the leather. So, the next question is, "how do I transfer my designs to the leather?"

Here, lay your leather and check the surface for any holes or uneven areas so you can carefully choose the leather part ideal for the work at hand. After that, trace out your designs and mark cut lines using a silver marking pen or pencil.

Alternatively, you use a pattern as a measuring guide for your project.

Leather working made easy

Cutting The Leather

How you cut your leather depends on the project at hand. Different designs require different cutting methods, but here is what you need to know.

Depending on the project, you can use scissors when working a thin leather, but a utility knife is better for cleaner cuts. However, leather shears are ideal, especially when following a template.

On the other hand, when working with thick leather or cutting curved areas, go for utility knives to get a clean cut. Lastly, use a strap cutter for projects like belts or pet collars because they are ideal for making accurate and consistent cuts on leather straps and belts.

Leatherworking and Crafting Techniques

After preparing and cutting your leather, let us get to the leatherworking and crafting techniques.

Dyeing leather

You can use any dye color for your leather, although the dyeing process works well on vegetable-tanned leather because it absorbs dyes easily. The purpose of dyeing leather is to make it look more attractive, though this does not have

Leather Working Made Easy

to be the case for all leather types. For example, full-grain leather becomes more beautiful as it ages, so you may want to maintain its natural color.

When purchasing dyes, there are a few options you can choose from;

- **Spirit-based dyes** penetrate deeply into the leather and give the leather an uneven look. The only disadvantage of spirit-based dyes is that they are not easily available.

- **Acetone-based dyes** rest on the surface of the leather with slight penetration. However, they evaporate rather quickly, so you need to ensure you dye your leather quickly and seal your bottles tightly after use.

- **Water-based dyes** give very bright results and are ideal for leather projects rarely exposed to bending or folding.

Skiving leather

Leather skiving involves reducing the thickness of leather using a leather skiver to even out the leather thickness to make it easy to bend and hide seams and folds. The leather skiver shaves off thin layers of leather material off the leather

Leather working made easy

surface or edges, resulting in improved project appearance and quality.

Gluing leather

Gluing is the process of joining two or more leather pieces using glue specially made for leather and suede. If the purpose of gluing is to have a temporary bond just to tack for stitching, use white glue as it is not permanent. If you want a permanent bond that does not require stitching afterward, use cement glue as it creates the most durable bonds.

Work in a well-ventilated workspace to avoid inhaling the chemical substance when working with glue. Also, ensure the leather surface you want to glue is clean and dry. For the best results, scratch or roughen the two leather surfaces you want to join, especially if they are very smooth and glossy. After applying the glue, make sure you leave it undisturbed for three hours to form the bond.

Burnishing leather

Burnishing is the process of smoothening rough edges by running a burnisher over the edges of the leather to give it an aesthetic appeal and protect the leather. To do it correctly, bevel and pre buff the edge with a damp cloth, then buff the edge using a burnisher until it is smooth to the touch.

46

Leather Working Made Easy

Saddle stitching

Saddle stitching is the most common method of stitching leather by hand, mainly because saddle stitches are strong and durable.

To saddle stitch, you need synthetic waxed nylon thread, which is the best for leatherworking, and two harness needles. The synthetic thread runs twice through the layers of leather, giving the stitch strength and durability.

To create a perfect saddle stitch, practice on leather pieces before you work on your main project.

Finishing leather

Applying finishes to the leather improves its overall quality and appearance. Here are more reasons why you need to apply leather finishes to leather;

- They protect the leather surface.

- They help enrich the colors of the dyes.

- They prevent the dyes applied on the leather from coming off and rubbing off on users.

- They make the leatherwork appear more professional.

- They keep mold from growing on leather surfaces.

Leather working made easy

Besides burnishing, below are other types of finishes applied to leather products.

Polishing

Polishing involves applying liquid, solid, or creamy substances that enrich leather. The good thing with polishing is that you can keep doing it, even with a finished project that's in use.

Make sure you clean the surface of the leather off all dust, debris, and dirt with a damp piece of cloth before you start polishing. If there is a lot of dust, use saddle soap with a cloth. Saddle soap consists of neat's-foot oil and is ideal for cleaning leather.

Oiling

Oiling involves applying oils like jojoba oil, mink oil, and shea butter oil on the leather surfaces to make them soft. The oils keep the leather from cracking and peeling due to dryness; they also enrich the pores of the leather giving it a rich look. Oiling also restores oils, especially if you use dyes that dry leather or buy already-dry leather.

Like every other type of finishing, you need to clean the leather surface before applying any oil to it.

Waxing

Waxing involves applying either solid or liquid wax onto the leather surface. However, liquid wax is the better option as it easily penetrates the leather pores and maintains its beauty. Applying wax on your leather surface helps give it a waterproof effect and finishes the leather edges.

When purchasing leather wax, go for the pure ones because it softens the leather and enriches the dye color.

Also, we have decorative techniques used in leather crafting such as;

Painting

Leather painting involves applying water-based acrylic paints that the leather pores then absorb. You can paint on both unfinished and finished leather.

Stamping

Leather stamping, also called engraving, involves pounding stamps onto the leather surface using a mallet to create imprints.

The best leather to practice stamping on is moist vegetable tanned leather because it is more workable than other leather materials. After stamping, waterproofing agents such as

Leather working made easy

waxes, oils, and polishes are applied to keep the shape and design from deforming or changing shape.

Shaping

This involves immersing the leather in water to make it more flexible, then shaping it using objects like a mallet. When it begins to dry, it stiffens and holds its shape.

Perforation

This decorative technique involves joining two pieces of leather to decorate them.

Pyrography

This involves using a hot needle or a leather burning tool to draw a shape on a leather surface. A hot needle creates darker leather drawings to form a complete picture.

Leather Working Made Easy

Chapter 6: Leather Pyrography

Leather pyrography involves decorating leather using a hot needle or a leather burning tool to engrave designs, writings, or drawings on the leather surface.

You may wonder, who invented this brilliant technique?

The ancient natives of Peru and Roman Britain are among the first said to have created objects using fire-heated metal rods, which they applied to wooden surfaces to create burned designs.

Also, during the Medieval, Renaissance, and Victorian periods, pyrography artists often used a portable stove and pot that had many holes in the lid, allowing the user to insert and heat sharp pokers used to burn designs onto leather pieces.

Leather pyrography has evolved over the years, with the tools evolving too to match the current technology. Another important thing is that you can burn designs on wood and engrave your designs on leather. With that brief history, let us now understand what we require to get started in leather pyrography.

Fortunately, you only require a few tools to get started. Here are the tools that you need.

51

Leather Burning Tool

This is a handheld tool with a burning tip that, when heated, creates the designs on the leather surface. The area near the tip is usually very hot, so ensure you hold the handle instead. Also, ensure that the handle is made of materials that do not conduct heat easily to avoid burning your hand and that the burning nib serves your purpose appropriately.

Another consideration when purchasing a leather heating tool is to get one with a heat regulator because leather does not require much heat to burn.

Designs Transfer Materials

Design transfer materials help you transfer designs and patterns onto your leather surface. They include;

Carbon paper

A carbon paper is a thin paper that's loosely bound with carbon or ink and used to transfer designs or images onto your leather. Simply place the carbon paper on the area you want your design, then use your leather burning tool to draw on top of the paper. The design will be on the leather surface when you remove your carbon paper.

Leather working made easy

Stencils

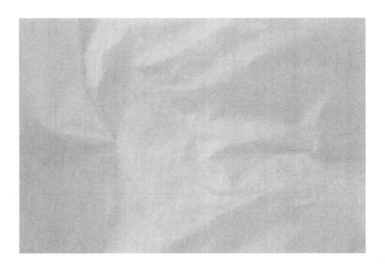

A stencil is a plastic, card, or metal sheet that is hollow cut and comes with a range of patterns, designs, or symbols that you can burn onto your leather.

Tracing paper

Leather Working Made Easy

Another way of transferring designs onto your leather is by using tracing paper on which you first sketch your designs then transfer them onto the leather piece.

Smooth surface

Leather pyrography requires that you work on a smooth surface to ensure you get a consistent burn. A cutting mat or a smooth wooden board can come in handy, especially since you also want to protect your working surface.

So, how do you burn leather?

When burning leather, go for vegetable tanned leather as it looks much better than the other leather materials. On the other hand, avoid using chemically tanned leather, but if you have to, make sure your workspace has enough ventilation because the chemicals in the leather can burn off, which can be dangerous for your health if inhaled.

It is best to purchase a burning tool with temperature control to regulate the heat when burning. However, you can still work with one that does not have temperature control, but in this case, you have to apply different pressures on different areas depending on your design.

To burn the leather, first dampen the material you are working on just enough to wet the surface, then place the

Leather working made easy

tracing material over your leather and use a scratch awl to transfer the image onto your leather. After tracing the design, take your burning tool and burn over the designs.

Tips to consider

- Do not stop halfway when using the burning tool; it creates a visible hole in the middle of the line.

- Keep your hand steady throughout to achieve clean burning marks.

- Clean the tip if it is not working as expected.

- Do not slant the burning tool too much because it can cause the rod to burn into the leather.

- Avoid using your fingers when unscrewing a hot tip because you can easily burn your fingers. Use a pair of pliers instead.

Leather Working Made Easy

Chapter 7: Leather Care And Maintenance Tips

No matter the form of your leather, you need to care for and maintain it. Here are ways that'll help ensure your leather lasts longer and stays in good shape.

Let your leather breathe

Leather comes from animals; therefore, it is a natural product that passes air through the pores on its surface. That said, your leather needs to have constant airflow to prevent rotting and mildew.

Avoid storing your leather in plastic bags since they do not allow any airflow; instead, use breathable fabrics like cotton to store the leather.

Avoid exposure to direct sunlight or heat

You may feel tempted to use a hairdryer to speed up the process of drying your bag because it is waterlogged; don't. When leather gets wet and exposed to heat too quickly, it shrinks and dries out fast.

Instead, let your items dry outside but in an area that does not receive direct sunlight. Also, avoid exposing any leather item to direct sunlight when storing it because the heat from

Leather working made easy

the sun's rays speeds up leather's fading process. The leather can also end up cracking and peeling. Instead, store your leather in darker places with some humidity.

Test your leather before applying anything

When using treatments such as polish or conditioner, always use a small area of the leather to do some testing first because these items may change the color of the leather depending on the brand.

For example, if you want to apply polish on your leather shoe, try testing a small area of your shoe, then give the polish 24 hours to see the results. If the shoe area does not change in color, you can comfortably apply the polish on both shoes. It is a lot of work, but you certainly do not want a shoe that looks different from what you expect.

Regular cleaning

Dirt, dust, and debris all lead to premature wear and peeling on any leather items, so it is good to regularly wipe them down with a damp piece of cloth or a paper towel as a way of preserving them.

Clean your leather at least once a week or every time you expose any leather item to winter snow. That way, you keep your leather items from premature aging. Also, condition

Leather Working Made Easy

your jackets every six months if you wear them regularly and whenever you notice some cracks or if the leather feels dry.

For leather furniture, do not use cleaning solvents, oils, furniture polish, or ammonia water; these products are harsh and speed up the wear and tear process. Instead, use vinegar mixed well with olive oil in a spray bottle.

Choose natural colors for creams and polishes

Most creams and polishes are either black, brown, or neutral in color. However, it is wise to go with natural colors to avoid unwanted colors changes brought on by using other colors. On the other hand, if the leather item is black, you can go ahead and apply black or brown polish or cream without changing its original color.

Waterproof once a year

This is not necessary because most leather products have undergone waterproofing agents treatin. However, if you are an active outdoors person, even during environmental conditions such as winter and heavy rains, consider waterproofing once a year. For example, if you are regularly out hiking with your boots in snow or heavy rains, you should waterproof in case the waterproofing agents wear off over time.

Leather working made easy

Chapter 8: Leatherworking Projects

This chapter will discuss some projects you can start on as a beginner, each with a detailed step-by-step guide and how you can fix any worn-out leather item.

Project 1: Leather Tool Case

Materials Needed:

- Zipper
- Leather
- Leather belt
- Fabric lining

Leather Working Made Easy

Steps

- Measure and cut out a parallelogram-shaped piece of leather. The corners should form angles approximately 98-degrees.

- Fold in the edges to form a rectangle, then add an iron-on stabilizer on the backside edge of the leather and iron the folded edges. The purpose of the iron stabilizer is to make the leather material stronger. Cut off the protruding edges after ironing.

- Mark some reference lines for the pockets using a groover.

- In this case, we use a machine for stitching, so after marking the reference lines, use dressmaker's pins to hold seams before stitching.

- Stitch the pockets in place.

- After stitching the pockets, cut another piece of leather to make an extra pocket for small items such as pencils and marker pens.

- Mark and cut the area for the zipper, then attach iron stabilizers on either side of the zipper using an iron.

Leather working made easy

Position the zipper using dressmakers' pins and stitch it in place.

- You can add your logo on the front of the pocket at this stage—use your custom-made decorative metal stamp.

- After adding the logo, topstitch it and keep the ends long so you can tie them at the back to make them more secure.

- Next, cut the fabric lining for the pocket using the dimensions of the leather piece you just stitched. Place the leather on the fabric with the wrong sides facing each other and include some allowance of about 1½-inches wide. Also, mark the fabric on the zipper area and cut.

- Stitch the lining around the zipper by hand using a lock stitch. Place this piece on another lining fabric piece with the same dimensions, mark the line along the leather edge to the lining pieces, then stitch a straight stitch one centimeter inside from the marked line. Add another straight stitch between the marked line and the straight stitch.

- Cut the excess lining to create a perfect-sized pocket.

Leather Working Made Easy

- You can also add a twill tape over the top edge of the pocket to give it a neat look.

- Finally, attach the pocket piece to the pocket roll you stitched earlier. Use clips to hold it in place while you stitch along the edges. Also, cut off excess leather from the ends of the belt.

- Punch holes on the belt for more of the needle to pass through, then attach it to the pocket roll, and voila! Your leather pocket roll is now complete, and you can add your leatherworking tools into the pockets.

Project 2: Leather Tote Bag

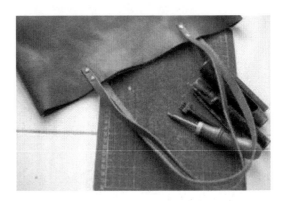

Materials Required:

- Brass rivets
- Leather

Steps

- Make patterns using your dimensions so the bag can be the perfect size for you. Mark two straight lines on both sides of your leather a ¼ inches from the edge of each height. Measure the depth of your bag from the lines and cut. Also, cut the bag straps using the excess leather material using a strap cutter. The straps are doubled; use white glue to tack them before stitching.

Leather Working Made Easy

- After cutting the straps, use a level-edged beveler to make curves on both ends, then use a leather chisel punch to make stitching holes on the straps. Also, burnish the straps' edges using beeswax and a piece of cloth and rub the straps until the spaces are closed.

- Next, punch holes for the brass rivets to go through on both the straps and bag body, depending on where you want the straps. The brass rivets are for attaching the straps to the bag.

- Next, attach your brass rivet, and in this case, we are doing it by hand, so use the images below to follow along.

- After attaching the rivets, mark the area for the pocket and cut out the pocket piece. In this case, the pocket is not a complete square, so use the grid on the cutting mat to measure and cut off about 1½ -inches from both sides of the bottom part of the pocket. Also, the stamping tool used is a custom-made decorative stamp to create a personal logo on the front of the pocket.

- Apply some white glue for a temporary tack before stitching, and use a chisel punch to make holes for stitching, then saddle stitch.

Leather working made easy

- Finally, stitch together the edges of your bag.

- Stitch the bottom edges and burnish them for a smooth finish.

- Finally, your leather tote bag is complete.

Project 3: Carved Leather Earrings

Materials required:

- Leather

- Earring hooks

In this case, the leather has carved designs, so we shall start with leather carving before making the earrings.

Steps

- First, cut out your earring pieces depending on your design and lay the patterns on the pieces. You can download the patterns from the internet for free and print them out.

Leather working made easy

- After transferring the patterns, take your swivel knife and make bold cuts on the patterns. You can attach layers of masking tape under your pieces to keep them from moving around when tooling.

- Next, take your beveler and mallet and bevel the carved patterns to give them a smooth and bolder look and add details to the patterns. Simply place the beveler on the patterns and pound the top with the mallet.

- Use a stamping tool with a vertical-lined thumbprint end to create the flower pattern. In this case, the middle of the flower is darker than the sides, so use your stamp and mallet to create the dark effect.

- Next, use your swivel knife to add line details to the patterns.

- That completes the carved earring pieces; now, we turn our attention to attaching the earring hooks. First, punch holes for the earring hooks using a leather hole punch for perfect round holes. If you have a leather punch set, use the smallest for punching and ensure the holes are in the same place on both earrings. After making the holes, use a chain nose

Leather Working Made Easy

plier to open the coil to the side, attach it to the earrings, then close it using the pliers.

Leather working made easy

Project 4: Leather Bracelet

Materials Required:

- Pattern
- Leather

Steps

- Transfer the pattern onto the leather and cut it out using a swivel knife.

- Curve the ends into a rounder shape, then mark the places where you want to make the holes. Use a punch with a smaller punching point to make the holes and pound on it with a mallet. Place a metal or wooden board below the leather to protect the working surface.

Leather Working Made Easy

- Apply wax to the edges and align them with sandpaper, then use a burnisher to give the edges a smooth look.

- Next, clean the leather with a damp woolen cloth and use a leather finishing spray to give your leather a rich look.

- Finally, install the clasp and fastener.

- After the clasp and fastener are in place, we need to add designs to the simple bracelet by burning on the leather. Here, take your leather burning tool, heat it, then burn the desired designs on your bracelets.

- You can make more bracelets and have a different design on each!

Leather working made easy

Project 5: Stamped and Dyed Leather Belt

Materials Required

- Leather
- Screws
- Buckle

Steps

- Cut a strip from your leather using your strap cutter, then measure out the side the buckle will be on by measuring approximately 3-inches from the edge. After that, mark another three inches from the mark, indicating where you begin the tooling.

- Next, measure out where the holes will be, and to do that, mark the area you want to buckle your belt from the first 3-inch mark you made using a pencil. That

Leather Working Made Easy

mark indicates where the buckle hole will be. Also, mark two holes 1-inch on either side of the buckle hole.

- After that, mark some inches from the buckle hole depending on how long you want the belt to be, then cut using a punch and a mallet.

- Next, using a wing divider, mark the border-line about ¼ inches from the edge to keep all your tooling within. You can also use a groover for this.

- Transfer your designs onto the leather. Here, we're drawing directly on the leather's surface using a pencil. You also need to dampen the leather and allow it to dry until it is almost back to its natural color, making it easier to hold the designs well. Next, take your stamping tools and stamp following the designs you already made.

- With the belt fully stamped, take your dye and brush, start coloring the areas you want to dye, and finish by oiling to give the belt some color. After that, you can let it rest for 15 minutes for the dye to settle in, then hand-stitch the border line and burnish all the edges for a smooth look.

Leather working made easy

- Next, we need to attach the buckle. To do this, we shall re-measure and mark the 3-inches from the end and halfway from the edge, which indicates where you will fold. Also, re-mark and punch two holes spaced 1-inch on either side of the hole and punch them out using a belt punch.

- Next, mark holes on the other side of the belt. To do this, line your tape measure from the buckle hole, measure your desired length, and punch the center from the edge indicating where the first hole will be. After that, punch two more holes from the first hole, each with a one-inch spacing.

- Next, put the screws on the buckle end, and to do that, attach them with the smooth side on top and then fold the buckle over so that you can attach the other end and tightly screw them. Finally, add the buckle, and your leather belt is complete!

Leather Working Made Easy

Project 6: Pyrographed Leather Wallet

Steps:

- First, cut out the patterns and trace them onto the leather surface using a scratch awl, then cut the pieces out using a swivel knife and a ruler for clean cuts.

- After cutting all the pieces, lay them out according to the order of assembly, then apply some beeswax to the edges and burnish them.

- Next, glue the small pocket onto the big pocket so you can stitch the inner seam; first, take the scratch awl and mark below the seam on both sides of the pockets to indicate where to glue up. Let the glue dry completely before attaching the pieces.

Leather working made easy

- After the glue dries up, line up the pieces with the edges as best as possible, press them intact using your fingers, then lightly pound the top using a hammer to set the glue. Ensure the hammer has a clean face so you cannot dent the leather.

- Next, take the seam you are stitching, level it using sandpaper, then use a size zero beveler to bevel the seams. Also, apply some beeswax to the seams and rub using a cloth.

- Next, mark the stitch line a ¼ inch from the seam edges using a wing divider. Also, use your chisel punch to create a mark where you will pass your needle through.

- After that stitch, the marked areas using synthetic nylon thread, and glue the pieces to the exterior.

- Next, use your calipers and chisel punch to mark the stitch line across the top, then back stitch on one end. After stitching, ensure you wax and burnish the edges.

- Next, we need to attach the final piece, the pie fold at the back, to the main piece to make the piece complete. To do this, punch holes on both pieces separately, then glue them together. After that, stitch

76

Leather Working Made Easy

the pieces together. Also, make sure you bevel and burnish the edges.

- Your wallet is not complete. The next step is to decorate the simple wallet using the leather burning technique. Transfer the patterns or designs onto the areas of the wallet you want to burn, heat your leather burning tool, then create the designs by moving the pyrography tool along the lines of the patterns.

- And your pyrographed leather wallet is complete!

Leather working made easy

Project 7: Leather Phone Case

Steps

- Transfer your patterns onto the leather and mark to size using a scratch awl.

- Use your set square to ensure the corners are square, then cut off the pieces using a swivel knife. After that, use glue to tack the pieces by applying glue on the back piece and not on the top part. Cut off the excess material.

- Next, mark the area for the belt and punch using an oblong punch and mallet.

Leather Working Made Easy

- Next, use your wing divider to mark the border line starting from the top of the oblong to just the other oblong. Mark around the belt hole too.

- After that, use your chisel punch and mallet to make the chisel line along the same line for stitching, then start stitching from the inner line going outwards, and finish with the other inner line along the oblong. When done with stitching, use the mallet to pound along the stitch line lightly for a neater look.

- Finally, you have completed your leather phone pouch and can wear it along your waist by sliding the belt through the holes.

Leather working made easy

Project 8: Leather Sunglasses Case

Steps

- In this case, we are using vegetable-tanned leather and shall dye it first. Take your leather dye, preferably oil dye, to help ensure your leather does not dry out. First, apply a thin coat of neat oil onto the leather's surface to restore some of the oils into the leather, then prepare your dye. After that, dip a woolen cloth into the dye and carefully dye your leather in circular motions. Apply at least three coats or until the dye evenly spreads on the leather.

- Give your dyed leather at least ten minutes to dry, then use a clean cloth to buff off any pigments that

Leather Working Made Easy

might still be on the surface, then gently massage neat foot oil again onto the leather to give it a rich look. Wear your gloves while at it.

- Download your pattern from the internet, print it on A4, then cut it out. Apply glue on thick paper and stick your pattern on it.

- Cut your pattern from the thick paper using scissors and trace it out on leather using a water-soluble mark pen. Cut your pattern from the leather.

- Next, apply glue to the back of the leather and lining then glue both pieces together. Trim the excess leather edges.

- After that, skive the leather edges, then use sandpaper or sand file to sand the edges. Also, apply beeswax and burnish the edges using a burnisher.

- Next, mark the location of the stitch and fastener holes. Use the groover to mark the stitch line, then use a double chisel punch to create the stitch holes. Also, punch a hole where you will attach the stub for fastening your case.

Leather working made easy

- Next, attach the stud, then fold the leather to confirm the location of the other hole where you also attach the stud. Punch the other hole and install the stud.

- Next, mark the punch holes for the leather strap, ensuring they are parallel to the stud screw. After that, punch holes to attach the straps, then install them using rivets.

- Next, fold the leather and make sure the stitch holes align, then first stitch the top curve edges as shown below to secure the lining.

- Continue stitching the folded edges together to form a complete piece.

- Finally, sand the leather edges and burnish them and your leather case is now complete.

Project 9: Leather Sandals

Materials required:

- Corks for shoe soling
- Soling sheets
- Veg tan leather
- Shoe leather lining
- Paints and brushes

Steps

- First, trace out your foot on card stock using a thin pen, ensuring you do not have the pen at an angle.

Leather working made easy

- Next, cut and put the masking tape on top of the foot approximately where you will have the straps, and make sure the tape has the same thickness as the straps. Mark where the straps cross the foot and add an inch to each strap measurement.

- Next, add 1/4-inches around the edges and use a French curve to curve the foot pattern.

- After cutting out the pattern, cut out the sole. First, cut out the lining that will touch the foot from strong leather lining that has minimal stretch, then glue it to a layer of cork or sole. The thickness of the cork depends on your measurements. Simply put on a layer of permanent shoemaking glue on both the lining and the cork, leave it for 15 minutes, then attach both pieces. You can also use a hammer with rounded edges and a smooth face to lightly pound on the pieces together for more security.

- Next, trim off the excess cork, use sandpaper to sand the edges, then burnish them with a burnisher.

- If you want your sandal to have a little height at the back, making the heel wedge is the next step. We make the wedge with cork material and a layer of leather

84

Leather Working Made Easy

lining by cutting the pieces to size and gluing the two together.

- Place a heavy object on the attached pieces to ensure a good attachment, then give them a few hours to dry. Once the glue dries, cut straight edges to make them equal. To turn the pieces into a heel wedge, mark a point from one edge, then mark another line 2-inches back from that point which indicates the position of the bevel.

- Next, use sandpaper to sand the bevel on both pieces using a belt sander or your hands.

- Next, measure and glue the heel wedge onto the sole. Trim down the excess cork and sand it using sandpaper to match the footbed.

- After that, measure and cut thick vegetable tanned leather to attach to the cork. It is good that you scrape off the leather pieces to ensure they can make a bond with the glue using a craft knife.

- Next, glue the vegetable-tanned leather and the cork, then starting from the back, attach the heel to the leather to the front. Let it dry for a few hours, then trim down the excess leather and sand it.

Leather working made easy

- Once done, trace out the outline of the sole, use the tracing to cut out the vegetable tan leather for the other sole, and repeat the same process for attaching it to the cork.

- Next, use a permanent marker to color the raw edge of the veg tan leather.

- To accommodate the straps, you need to cut off a portion of the veg tan leather, so make sure the leather you use is thick. Mark the area you will attach the strap and cut away a portion of it.

- Next, measure and cut your leather straps from medium-weight shoemaking leather with close to zero stretch capacity and carefully cut the fuzzies off. First, attach one side of the straps, place your foot on the sole, measure and mark on your strap where you will attach it on the other side of the sole. Before attaching the strap, use a skiving knife to thin out the portions beneath the shoe so that they do not leave bumps.

- Do the same with all four straps.

- With the straps in place, the sandals are almost complete, with one final step involving installing the soling sheets to the bottom of the sandals. First, use

Leather Working Made Easy

sandpaper to rough up the sides of leather straps attached to the sole, then use the sole measurements to cut the sheets. After that, rough the sides that you will then glue the bottom part of the sandals and the sheets.

- Finally, install the soling sheet, trim off the excess edges, and smooth out the edges with sandpaper.

- And with that, your leather sandals are done, although they need a little bit of color; we shall paint the straps for a more appealing look.

- Gather your leather paint and finisher, then clean your leather straps with a damp piece of cloth in readiness for painting. Also, apply the deglazer and let it dry for a few minutes. After the deglazer dries, take your brush and paints of desired colors and apply thin, even layers on areas you want to paint. Also, you cover the shoe areas you do not want to paint with masking tape to protect them.

Once done with the painting job, let the paint dry for 15-20 minutes or until it no longer feels tacky to your fingers.

- Finally, apply leather cream or polish to rehydrate the leather to give it a shine. And your sandals are done!

Leather working made easy

Project 10: Simple Leather Pouch

Materials required:

- Rivets

- Veg tan leather

Steps

- In this case, it is a small pouch that fits a phone and maybe a couple more items, so start by measuring and marking on a copy paper first. Mark a few inches using your set square on both ends and make a line using a straight ledge as shown.

- Use your square to measure and mark three more lines vertically. Add an inch at one end for the flap.

- Using a swivel knife, cut out your pattern and scribble out the lines again.

Leather Working Made Easy

- Fold your pattern along the lines and mark each section to avoid confusion when transferring the pattern onto the leather.

- Next, lay your pattern out on the leather surface, mark, then cut out the leather piece. Also, use the pattern to mark the bends.

- Next, use the curve of a round object to measure and cut the top curve of the snap. You can do this by folding the pattern and placing a round object at the fold to mark a curve.

- Also, mark the position of the snap fastener and punch the top hole using a revolving punch, and the bottom hole using a belt punch.

- Next, add the snap fasteners to the leather.

- With the bend marks in place, apply glue on the pocket part, fold, and hold in place using clips. Let it settle for five minutes.

- Next, mark and punch holes using a revolving punch set at the smallest punch.

- After that, attach the double cap rivets onto the punched holes. Take the rivet and push them through

Leather working made easy

the holes from the back, then install the rivet caps from the front of the project.

- And your leather pouch is done. You can paint on whatever you want to give it a better look.

Project 11: Pencil Case

Materials Required:

- Zipper
- Leather

Steps

- Cut your pattern from thick leather, trace it out on the leather, then skive the leather edges.

- Next, sand the leather edges using sandpaper, then burnish them using a burnisher until you see shiny edges. Take the leather pieces and mark the stitch line using a groover.

- Apply double-sided tape to the zipper and leather edges, then remove. The tape leaves glued surfaces when removed.

Leather working made easy

- Next, stick the zipper to leather, taking your time with the curved edges. You can use an awl to achieve better results at the corners. Make sure the center of your zipper's slider body is at the middle line of the main leather so that when transferring the patterns to the leather, mark the middle.

- Keep aligning the edges until the zipper is neatly in place.

- Place your pattern on leather, mark where to punch the first stitch hole, then punch the stitch holes using a chisel punch and a mallet. Adjust the zipper slider body to avoid punching it when punching the center part.

- Next, saddle stitch the edges and trim the threads off.

- Mark stitch holes using an awl for the side leather and straight stitch line on the main leather, then punch the stitch holes.

- Make small notches at the curved edges of the side leather to help make your stitching easier. Ensure you do not cut all the way to the stitch hole.

- Next, stitch side leather and main leather together and trim the thread off. Also, trim uneven edges, sand

Leather Working Made Easy

them with sandpaper, then apply finishing cream and burnish the edges.

- Finish by applying edge dye to the edges, and that's it!

Leather working made easy

Project 12: Leather Key Holder

Materials required:

- Leather
- Alphabet stamps or logo stamps
- Leather rivets
- Keyring

Steps

- Start by cutting out the leather according to your dimensions and pattern and smooth down the edges using sandpaper.

Leather Working Made Easy

- Punch holes for rivets or screws in both pieces, depending on your preference.

- Use your stitching groove to make a stitching line on both pieces and bevel the edges with an edge beveler.

- Dampen the leather pieces and stamp your logo or use alphabet stamps to create your name or a name you prefer. In this case, we have a custom-made logo.

- After the leather dries up, apply a little finishing oil to protect your leather and give it a natural look.

- Next, apply cement glue at the back of each piece, attach the pieces together, then make stitching holes using either a hand stitching chisel punch or a regular stitching chisel.

- Next, saddle stitch the project following the stitching holes. You can hold the project using a stitching horse while making the stitches so you can comfortably work with both hands.

- Apply beeswax to the edges, then burnish them with a burnisher.

- After that, attach the keyring and secure it with a rivet or screw.

Leather working made easy

- And you are done

Project 13: Leather Plant Hanger

Materials required:

- Metal ring
- Rivets
- Metal shaft
- Leather

Steps

- Lay out the leather, then measure out four strips using a ruler and a pen. Make sure you draw on the back so that the pen marks are not visible on the front.

Leather working made easy

- Next, take your leather shears and cut out the strips.

- Mark punch holes at the ends of each of your strips and punch out the holes using a revolving punch.

- Lay out the leather strips in a cross shape. Take the shaft part of your rivet and push it through the four holes, then take the cap and secure it on top.

- Take a plastic mallet and give the top of the rivet a gentle tap twice to secure it.

- Next, join all the strips of leather together at the top. Get a shaft, take the first strip, press the shaft over the top, and do the same to the remaining three strips. Ensure the front of the leather faces the top when attaching the shaft to keep the planter from getting twisted.

- Next, get the small strip, push the shaft through one hole with the back side facing up, then fold it and attach the other hole with the back side facing up. After that, press the rivet tap onto the top. Use a mallet to hammer it down for more security.

Leather Working Made Easy

- Next, get your metal ring, bend it open, get it through the loop, and finally add a hook for hanging. And your plant hanger is done!

Leather working made easy

Project 14: Leather Dog Collar

Materials Required:

- D-ring
- Buckle
- Bridle butt
- Looping
- Veg tan leather

Steps

- Cut your strip of leather from veg tan leather and square out the end using a set square.

Leather Working Made Easy

- Next, cut an egg point on one end.

- Mark holes from the egg point, with the first hole two inches from the end and the other four holes, 1-inch apart. Using a tape measure, measure and mark the overall measurement of your dog collar from the point.

- Mark two inches from the other end. From the egg point, mark 5½ inches, then bevel the edges. Also, skive two wedges from the end that you marked two inches.

- Next, stain and polish the leather mark out the crude punch holes using dividers, then use your crew punch to punch all the way.

- Next, temporarily attach the buckle, mark the stitch line, then mark the stitch holes.

- Next, skive the egg point a little. Wrap the strap around the collar, mark where its end meets the long end of the looping, then assemble the dog collar by attaching the buckle with the wedges on either side of the buckle. Tack them in place with nails.

- Next, saddle stitch the edges.

Leather working made easy

- Stain and polish the edges of the buckle area so they can blend with the rest of the layers.

- Even your holes for the collar using a divider, then punch them out using a revolving punch, and your dog collar is ready.

Project 15: Leather Mouse Pad

Materials Required:

- Leather
- Stamping tools

Steps

- Lay out a piece of copy paper, measure and mark the length and width of your mouse pad, then cut out the pattern. Next, take a round object, mark the curved edges, then cut.

- Transfer the pattern onto the leather using a marker pen or pencil, then cut it out using a swivel knife.

Leather working made easy

- Next, take your beveler and bevel the edges, then make a stitch line using a groover. Be careful when grooving the corners.

- Next, create the border stamp to create a unique look. First, case your leather by wetting it a little using a brush and water to make the stamping easier.

- After that, take your stamping tools and create the border stamp. We have the veiner stamp and continuous mule's foot stamping tool in this case.

- Continue pounding the stamping tools with a mallet until the border stamp is complete.

- Give the leather two hours to dry, then add some dye. In this case, we are using oil dye because it does not leave the leather dry. Apply three or four layers of dye, doing your best to spread it evenly.

- Give the dye 1½ hours to dry nicely, then apply antique leather finish by rubbing it gently using a piece of cloth. Wipe off the excess gel and buff the leather surface with a clean, dry piece of cloth.

- Next, take a cotton cloth and sparingly and evenly spread a wax-based topcoat onto the leather surface.

Leather Working Made Easy

Give it a few minutes to dry, then buff the leather with a dry cotton cloth.

- Next, apply cement glue to the backside of the leather and suede, then attach the suede piece to give the mouse pad body. Simply use the leather piece to cut out the suede to size, then attach both pieces. Use a mallet to give the pieces a more secure attachment.

- Finally, apply wax to the edges and burnish them, and your leather mouse pad is complete.

Leather working made easy

Project 16: Leather Cord Keeper

Materials Required

- Rivets
- Leather

Steps

- First, transfer your pattern onto the leather surface and cut the pieces out using a swivel knife.

- Using a U-shape strap punch and mallet, cut out curves on both ends of each piece. Apply wax to the edges, then use a burnisher to burnish the edges.

- Next, use an awl to create holes for inserting the leather snap fasteners, then punch them out using a rotary punch.

Leather Working Made Easy

- Next, attach the snap fasteners onto the leather pieces. Make sure that you secure them with a snap setter.

- Do the same to all pieces.

- And now your leather cord keepers are done, so you can go ahead and attach the cords.

Leather working made easy

Project 17: Leather Bottle Holder

Materials Required:

- Veg tan leather
- Bottle

Leather Working Made Easy

Steps

- Start by making a pattern. Simply place the bottle of choice on a copy paper and draw around the base. Next, use a ruler to cut out medium-height strips.

- Next, place the pieces together to form a cross, then place the centerpiece in the middle.

- Next, place your complete pattern onto the leather surface and trace it out using an awl.

- Cut out the leather pieces using a swivel knife.

- Next, use a sand file to sand the edges of the pieces, then bevel them using a beveler.

- After that, take your mink oil and give the pieces a coating of the oil.

- Next, take your U-shape strap punch and mallet and create curved ends on the main piece.

- Apply beeswax to the edges and burnish them using a burnisher.

- Next, take your base and main piece, then mark the stitching line and punch out the stitching holes.

Leather working made easy

- Apply glue on the backside of both pieces and attach them, then pound with a mallet to give them a tight attachment.

- Next, thread your needle and stitch all the way round, then trim the threads.

- With the base complete, take your clips and use them to hold the other pieces together to form the shape of the bottle holder.

- Take the short side straps and install the rings. Simply fold two inches from one end, slide the ring through, then punch stitching holes and stitch.

- Next, temporarily install the fasteners onto the long holding straps, then mark rivets holes. Remove the fasteners and punch the holes using a rotary punch.

- Install the rivets.

- Next, install the rivets onto the main piece to secure the center strap to the base piece.

- Assemble all the parts to form a complete piece. Simply attach the fastener of the top piece to the ring on the bottom piece.

- And your bottle holder is done!

Project 18: Leather Valet Tray

Steps

- Lay out your leather on the work surface, and using a ruler and an awl, mark the width and length of your valet tray.

- Use your swivel knife or cutting wheel to cut out the leather piece.

- Fold the piece from the edges to form a triangle, then hold the ends using clips. Next, measure one inch from the corner edge and mark holes using a double teethed punch. Mark and punch holes for all corners.

- Next, thread your needles and saddle stitch from the point you punched your holes as shown but do not

Leather working made easy

stitch to the end. Ensure you fold the leather with the finished side facing up.

- Do the same for all corners. And your leather valet tray is complete.

- Alternatively, you can attach rivets to the corners if you do not want to do stitch work.

Leather Working Made Easy

Project 19: Leather Double Wrap Cuff

Materials Required:

- Rivets

- Buckle

- Floral stamping tool

Steps

- Take your tape measure, wrap it around your wrist, measure, then double the measurements because it is a double rap.

- Next, you will need an oblong for inserting the buckle tongue. Take your leather and mark two holes on one

Leather working made easy

end for attaching the rivets when installing the buckle tongue.

- From the middle of your oblong, mark the size measurements of your double wrap cuff and mark, then mark three more holes from the mark you just made. To do this, back in a ½ -inch and mark, and go out two more halves and again, mark giving a total of four holes.

- Next, punch all the holes you marked using a rotary punch.

- Using a U-shape strap punch, make a belt tip on your cuff strap.

- Use an oblong punch to punch a hole for your buckle.

- Next, stamp your leather cuff using a floral stamp to give it a beautiful look but first, case your leather lightly using a brush and water. To create your stamps, simply place your floral stamping tool on the area you want the design, and pound on it using a mallet.

- Next, add some antique pieces to the leather to give it a dark effect. Simply use a buffer to rub the antique gel

Leather Working Made Easy

properly on the leather without leaving the stamped areas.

- Take a cotton cloth and wipe off the excess gel, then give it an hour to dry.

- Next, take your wax and lightly coat the strap using a buffer, then buff it using a clean piece of cotton cloth. Buff the strap until it is dry.

- Next, install the rivets and buckle. First, set the buckle in place by sliding the buckle tongue through the oblong, then take your double cap rivets and attach them to the rivet holes you punched earlier.

- And your double strap cuff is done.

Leather working made easy

Project 20: Leather Clutch Bag

Materials Required:

- Snap fasteners

- Veg tan leather

Steps

- Download the clutch bag pattern from the internet and print it on A4 copy paper. Websites like pinterest.com have clutch bag patterns that you can download and print if you do not want to go the old-school way of making your pattern from scratch.

- Next, cut along the outer line of the pattern.

- Next, trace out the pattern and cut out the outer and inner pieces.

Leather Working Made Easy

- Apply adhesive glue over the backside of both pieces.

- Give the glue five minutes to dry, then attach the pieces.

- Attach the pattern and mark the holes using an awl.

- Next, cut the edges using a circular punch.

- With the pattern still on the leather, cut all lines according to the pattern.

- Remove the pattern after cutting, smooth the edges using sandpaper, then add a creasing line to all the edges.

- Next, mark a stitch line using a divider and make stitch holes using a chisel punch.

- Saddle stitch all the way around.

- Next, bevel the edges with a beveler, then coat them with dye. Also, apply wax to the edges and burnish them.

- You can also add your customized logo to the top part.

- Cut leather straps for the clutch bag using your pattern and curve the ends using a curved punch.

Leather working made easy

- Also, cut a piece to attach to the end of the strap, skive one end, and coat with adhesive glue.

- Apply glue to the end of the straps too, attach the piece, then cut and trim the edges.

- Make the crease line along the edges of the straps, then use your divider to make the stitch line. Next, punch the stitch holes using a chisel punch.

- Next, bevel the edges, coat them with some dye, then burnish them.

- Mark and punch holes on the straps and main body for inserting the snap fasteners.

- Attach the snaps on both the straps and main body.

- Next, mark the area on the main body you want to attach the strips and coat with adhesive glue. Coat the strips with glue, then attach them to the main body.

- Punch the stitch holes with a small awl, then saddle stitch.

- Next, punch holes for attaching snap fasteners and install the snaps to each position.

Leather Working Made Easy

- Finally, fold the leather, shape it, and fasten the snaps according to their respective positions.

- And your leather clutch bag is done.

Leather working made easy

Project 21: Leather Flask

Steps

- Start by cutting your leather to size by simply measuring the width and length of your flask then using the dimensions to cut out the leather. You can add your customized logo at this stage.

- Next, use your wing dividers to create a stitch line for decorative stitching, then use your chisel punch to punch the stitching holes.

- Saddle stitch.

Leather Working Made Easy

- Next, attach the leather to the flask. Start by taping off the top and bottom edges of the flask. To attach the leather to the flask, apply a coat of adhesive glue on the backside of the leather and the flask, wait for it to dry, then stick them together. Ensure you carefully align the horizontal and vertical center of the flask.

- Once done, flip the flask over and carefully wrap each side of the leather around the flask.

- Next, cross stitch the two edges meeting at the center.

- And with that, the flask is done.

Leather working made easy

Project 22: Minimalist Wallet

Steps

- Make a pattern as shown using your dimensions.

- Trace out the pattern onto your leather surface using an awl, then punch an awl at the intersection to avoid future tears, before you cut out the pattern.

- Next, use your swivel knife to cut out the pattern. To cut out the thumb slot, use a ¾- inch punch for the curves or your swivel knife if you do not have one.

- Next, burnish all the edges, including the thumb slot.

- After that, glue the parts together. First, make a mark at the intersection so you can know where exactly to glue.

Leather Working Made Easy

- Start gluing the first two backsides together.

- Before assembling the other part, scratch the smooth leather surface using a scratch awl so that the glue bonds better.

- Next, glue the parts you are joining together using adhesive glue and press them together.

- Next, use sandpaper to sand the edges, then use your divider to mark the stitch line. After that, make punch holes using your chisel punch.

- Stitch and trim the edges.

- Bevel the edges using a beveler. Also, apply leather wax to the edges and burnish them.

- And with that, your simple two-side leather wallet is done.

Project 23: Leather Pen Case

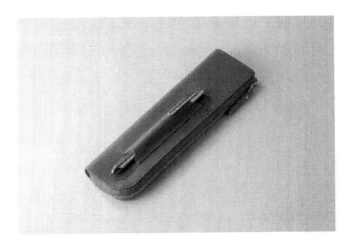

Materials Required:

- Rivets
- Leather

Steps

- Download pen case pattern from the internet and print it on A4.

- Use a swivel knife to cut your pattern from the copy paper, then apply glue on thick paper and glue your pattern.

- Cut your pattern from the thick paper and trace it on leather using an awl or erasable mark pen.

Leather Working Made Easy

- Next, cut the pattern from leather using a swivel knife and semi-round punch to help trim the inner area.

- Place your pattern on the cut piece and mark snap holes and stitch holes according to your pattern.

- Bevel the leather edges using a beveler, then sand the inner edges. After that, apply burnishing cream to the inner edges and burnish them.

- Fold the inner protruding section as shown and punch a hole for installing the snap fastener.

- Next, install the snaps.

- Next, mark the stitch line using a groover, then apply glue on the edges of both leather pieces.

- Join the pieces together, ensuring the edges align properly.

- Next, punch stitch holes using a chisel punch.

- Lock both needles with thread and stitch along the stitch holes. Make sure you trim the thread when done.

Leather working made easy

- Bevel the edges, then sand them using sandpaper. After that, apply finish cream or wax to the edges and burnish.

- Next, punch a hole on the flap for snap installation, then install the snap fastener.

- Snap your fastener closed, and your project is now complete.

Project 24: Leather Flip Flops

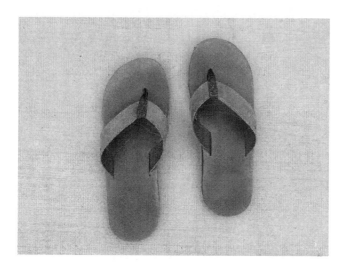

Steps

- Start by tracing your foot on a copy paper to make a pattern and add 3/8-inches for stitching.

- Punch a hole on the pattern for the strap.

- Next, place the pattern on the leather and cut three layers for each flip flop. Also, cut out the thongs and straps.

- Next, cut the liner for the thongs from pigskin leather because it is more durable. After cutting, glue the backsides of the thong and liner.

Leather working made easy

- Make slits on the straps so you can fold the center back and sand the edges of the straps. Also, use a groover to make the stitching line, then punch stitching holes using a chisel punch.

- With the glue dry, stick the strap and the liner together and slightly pound them using a mallet for a stronger attachment.

- Next, saddle stitch the straps together.

- Trim the edges of the thongs and sand them flat. Also bevel the edges and mark stitch holes using a chisel punch.

- Next, dye the thongs using alcohol dye and add a touchmark to the side of the thong.

- Next, place the pattern on the sole and mark where the strap and the thongs will attach. Punch a hole for the strap and use the oblong punch for the thong holes.

- Cut out sections on the sole lining where the straps and thongs sit.

- Glue the backside of the sole and lining and attach the pieces together.

Leather Working Made Easy

- Next, dye the straps on both sides.

- Saddle stitch the liner to the thong along the punched stitch holes.

- Glue the section you cut on the sole and attach the straps, then make stitching holes using an awl. Saddle stitch along the marked holes, then apply beeswax and burnish the back of the strap so it does not rub the area between your toes in a way that it may wound it.

- Sand the edges of the thong flat, then burnish them until you get the desired result.

- Next, dye the soles using the same dye as the straps and thongs.

- Mark stitching lines and holes on the sole for the thongs.

- Also, align the strap with the thong and mark more stitching holes.

- Next, assemble the parts and apply glue on the thong where you will attach the strap. Also, pass the ends of the thongs through the hole you created, stitch the two ends together, then glue the third layer of the sole.

Leather working made easy

- Next, sand the edges of the flip flops, apply wax, then burnish them.

- Also bevel the edges using a beveler.

- Now mark stitch line on the soles of the flip flops and stitch holes, then saddle stitch.

And your flip-flops are done!

Leather Working Made Easy

Conclusion

The main reason for writing this book is to help you as a reader understand that leather products are not only machine-made but that as a beginner, there are several projects you can do yourself right in the comfort of your home!

Each chapter takes you through the basics of leatherworking and crafting in a way that helps you understand what working with leather is all about.

Read each chapter carefully because there is more than just getting into the projects. The book also helps you understand leather as a material so you can make choices based on know-how rather than guesswork.

Finally, the book has easy do-it-yourself leather crafting projects you will probably enjoy making. This book is especially ideal for beginners because each project has detailed steps guiding you on working your way through the specific project.

Whether you are an aspiring leather craftsman or a leatherwork hobbyist, I hope this book will really help you and offer you real value.

Leather working made easy

PS: I'd like your feedback. If you are happy with this book, please leave a review on Amazon.

Please leave a review for this book on Amazon by visiting the page below:

https://amzn.to/2VMR5qr

Printed in Great Britain
by Amazon